LET WISDOM SPEAK
KEYS to FULFILL YOUR DESTINY

Wisdom Principles & Journal

By

TERRY D. GARTRELL

COPYRIGHT

LET WISDOM SPEAK:

KEYS to FULFILL YOUR DESTINY

Wisdom Principles & Journal

© **Copyright 2019 by Terry D. Gartrell**

ISBN- 9781705507537

Editor: At the Table Life Coaching & Motivational Speaking Services LLC

All rights reserved. Printed in the United States of America. No part of this book or parts thereof may reproduced in any form, stored in a retrieval system, or transmitted in any form by any means – electronic, mechanical, photocopy, recording, or otherwise without prior written expressed permission from NuVision Counseling & Coaching Solutions or Terry D. Gartrell, legal representative. Brief quotations in printed reviews are permissible.

All Scripture quotations are from the New King James Bible, New International Version, Amplified Bible, and New American Standard Bible translations and are public domain in the United States.

Printed in the United States of America

DEDICATION

This book is dedicated to all those who have made multiple mistakes and they may think God has forgotten about them. This book is dedicated to those who cannot begin to imagine why they were born, as well as to those who have been told, "You will never be anything" or "You do not have what it takes." Maybe you have tried something and failed. Maybe you feel abandoned or betrayed, and just cannot seem to shake it and move forward. Can I tell you that before you were formed in your mother's womb, God knew your end from the beginning? (Isaiah 46:10). Be blessed as you read this book and implement the principles. A wise man once said, "When the student is ready, the teacher will appear." My prayer is that as you work through this book, your life will transform for the better.

LET WISDOM SPEAK:

KEYS to FULFILL YOUR DESTINY

Wisdom Principles & Journal

ENDORSEMENT

I celebrate with my wife, Terry, as she is encouraging others with hope for change, as she shares wisdom principles and guides the readers to connect with their higher selves. She is transparent as she shares a part of her testimony. Readers will be able to "feel" the transformation as they move forward with the steps to fulfill their purpose and destiny. I am very proud of my wife, and I believe this book will help you make progress.

Sammy L. Gartrell

ACKNOWLEDGEMENTS

First and foremost, I thank God who is the head of my life, for sending His servants across my path when I thought I would not make it. Thank you for instilling in me a new hope and courage to embrace that which you called me to do while I was yet in my mother's womb (Jeremiah 29:11). Thank you for blessing me to be a blessing.

I thank:

My children Kristian and Vincent II, and my beautiful granddaughters - Jordyn Ericka and Janibeth

My mother, Betty for giving me life and giving me space to grow and become my own person

My grandmother, Alberta for nurturing me and building a strong foundation of prayer in me

My faithful friend and prayer partner: Angelique Summerset

I am thankful for friends and family who encouraged me along the way:

Lillie Braswell
Norma Clark
Rechelle Wynn
Tangela Flemming
Karen Wells
The E3 Family

Spiritual Mentors who help to shorten the distance or spoke life to me:

Bishop Stanley Williams, who over 16 years ago, prophesied that God would use me to help people fulfill their potential. Father I thank you tremendously. Just one Word can change your life. Bishop Jordan, who God used to enlighten me along my journey and shift me into my destiny. I finished my education, and talents have been uncovered.

Pastor Mascareen Cohen for encouraging me to press my way

Brenda Bryant who encouraged me, prophesied to me, prayed with me, and did not judge me

My prayer partners:

Lillie Braswell
Angelique Summerset
Brenda Bryant
Norma Clark
Carla Harvey
Tangela Flemming
Rechelle Wynn
H.T. Brock
Icilda Hogan

I would also like to acknowledge Prophet Antoine Jasmine, Pastor Brian Butler, Sally London, the late Prophet Devon Thompson, Prophetess Antoinette Harris, Karen Wells, Anthony Butler, Pastor Theresa Stanford, and the late Dr. Suzan Armstrong-West, who God used in His own way to remind me of His promises.
I want to thank two very special people I have met as my book was in process.
- My husband, Sammy Gartrell for his loving support
- J. Dianne Tribble for her inspiration, even when she did not know it and for providing her wisdom and insight on helping this project come to fruition

Table of Contents

Page Number:

Preface	1
The Principles	
Principle 1: Believe in the Vision	3
Principle 2: Change Your Thinking	13
Principle 3: Be True to Yourself and God	25
Principle 4: Be Grateful for All Things	31
Principle 5: Believe Success is for You and Recognize Opportunity	39
Principle 6: Have Courage to Prepare	45
Principle 7: Walk in the Fullness Thereof	51
About the Author	57
Contact the Author	59

PREFACE

This book is my testimony of how God used a major event to activate the unveiling of my purpose and identity. Many times, when people encounter trials and tribulations, they give up and some never recover. When I separated from my husband, Vincent, and eventually divorced, I completely gave up hope. How was I to raise my two children? I sunk in a deep depression, briefly turned away from God, and became hopeless. Eventually, I became so angry and rebellious that I began to lash out at anybody I felt was taking advantage of me.

Finally, after an altercation with a roommate, I found myself facing the possibility of losing my freedom. She had taken advantage of me. At that point, I definitely had no strength or ability to defend myself. But God…. It was during that period that I truly surrendered and began to cry out to God for healing and deliverance. During that time, God Himself lifted me out of the pit, brushed me off, and began to mold me into the woman of God He called me to be.

It certainly has been a journey, but can I tell you that God can do anything but fail. If you are reading this book today, know this: God can and will fulfill His purpose in your life. Wait on Him, and don't give up. I pray that the Spirit of the living God will rest upon you and empower you to finish the course, as He reveals the true you. In Jesus' Name. Amen.

~ Terry D. Gartrell

2

Principle One: Believe in the Vision

For the vision is yet for an appointed time; But at the end it shall speak… Habakkuk 2:3 (NKJV)

People of all ages wonder what their purpose is, and yet at times when God begins to reveal their purpose to them, they do not believe Him. When I was going through the tough times of single parenting, having little or no support, and being rejected, I still had to believe. Although at times the circumstances or situations dictated otherwise, I still had to believe. When friends and family did not understand or spoke ill of me, I still had to believe. No matter what the facts were, I still had to believe. When others did not believe, guess what? I still had to believe. When I had not been affirmed or confirmed, even then, I yet had to believe. I had to believe because without doing so, we cannot obtain God's promises for our lives.

God will show you what His plan is for your life when you are in relationship with Him. Once He does this, you must agree with what Heaven says about your final outcome. This means your thoughts, actions, and emotions need to come into alignment. Remember, God knows the end from the beginning (see Isaiah 46:10).

When I began to consider what material I wanted to publish first, I began to think about my strengths. In the past, I was not good at staying focused and on task in the midst of transition or challenge. However, when I began to understand that all things work together for my good (Romans 8:28), my entire mindset began to change.

God always has purpose for anything He does or anything He allows. Trust Him.

There is an old saying that states, "What doesn't kill you will make you stronger." As simple as it may sound, it is true. The problem is, we do not like pain. We do not like going through the process. We absolutely detest not being in control. Always remember that there are no shortcuts in life. Nobody can give you the answers to the test. You must go through the process and pass the test.

Affirmation: I shall do all that God has called me to do.

Principle One: Believe in the Vision
Journal Writing Prompt

What do you see as your **strengths**? Explain your strengths and how they have impacted you and others up to this point in your life.

Principle One: Believe in the Vision
Journal Writing Prompt

What do you see as your **weaknesses**? Explain your weaknesses and how they have impacted you and others up to this point in your life.

Principle One: Believe in the Vision
Journal Writing Prompt

How has the **pain** of your experience(s) influenced you as a person?

Principle One: Believe in the Vision

Journal Writing Prompt

What is your **vision** for your life?

Principle One: Believe in the Vision

Journal Writing Prompt

How has your **life experience(s)** influenced your vision?

Principle One: Believe in the Vision
Journal Writing Prompt

How important do you think it is to have a **vision** for your life?

Principle One: Believe in the Vision

Journal Writing Prompt

Please take a moment to write down your **short-term goals**. These are goals you will work to complete within the next 12 months. Please make sure you list a projected date of completion.

12

Principle Two: Change Your Thinking

Be ye transformed by the renewing of your mind...Romans 12:2 (KJV)

As I continued to pursue my education as a mental health practitioner, I realized I was indeed being elevated to another level-both personally and professionally. One way in which I have seen profound change come into my life experience is through the awareness of the power we possess mentally. It seems so simple, yet it can be complex. For years, most of us are taught to focus on negativity and by doing so, we actually magnify or multiply negativity in our experiences.

So, how does one go through the process of transformation? One way is to embrace the spiritual principles in Scripture. In addition, we can also change our perspective on things. In the field of psychology, it is called reframing. With deliberate effort and diligence, we can retrain our mind, the subconscious-------- the area of our mind that contains all the messages we receive throughout our lives. The subconscious deals with involuntary actions. I call it "Being on auto pilot."

The problem is, when we began to ruminate and replay self-defeating thoughts or memories over and over again, that too is reflected in our actions. The beauty of this is that we can reprogram our brains through techniques such as affirmations, visualization, and meditation. Since I have started integrating these and other techniques, I am more centered, peaceful, and productive. When chaos is absent, quite naturally, we accomplish more.

If you are a skeptic, I challenge you to put into practice some or all the techniques I have mentioned. I guarantee, you will be amazed. Remember, your thoughts become your actions. You must become very intentional about your life. When you do so, you will find that you do not have time or energy to waste on people, places, or things that do not align with the vision. I challenge you to write down a plan for your life. Take the limits off and write. You are shifting.

Affirmation: I have clarity of thought which causes my life to change for the better.

Principle Two: Change Your Thinking
Journal Writing Prompt

How has your thinking caused you to self-sabotage? Be specific.

Principle Two: Change Your Thinking
Journal Writing Prompt

What can you do today to start the process of shifting your thinking? For example, daily affirmations?

Principle Two: Change Your Thinking

Journal Writing Prompt

What thought patterns are you holding on to in which you feel are preventing you from transforming and reaching your full potential (long term)?

Principle Two: Change Your Thinking
Journal Writing Prompt

Are there any negative thought patterns that are hindering your daily functioning (short term)? If yes, what are they?

Principle Two: Change Your Thinking
Journal Writing Prompt

Are there any negative thought patterns that are hindering you intra-personally? If yes, what are they?

Principle Two: Change Your Thinking
Journal Writing Prompt

How has this chapter impacted your thought process?

Principle Two: Change Your Thinking
Journal Writing Prompt

Are you able to identify any cognitive distortions you use?

Principle Two: Change Your Thinking
Journal Writing Prompt

Why is it so important to renew your mind on a daily basis?

Principle Two: Change Your Thinking
Journal Writing Prompt

What practices do you use to renew your mind? Please explain in detail.

Principle Three: Be True to Yourself and God

For I know the plans I have for you," declares the LORD, "plans to prosper you and not to harm you, plans to give you hope and a future...Jeremiah 29:11 (NIV)

Why is it that we say one thing and do another? Believers are notorious for this. When we act in ways that are incongruent with our core beliefs, ultimately, we become miserable, stagnated beings. The reason this happens is because we essentially are living a double life. We settle for less than God's best for us - somehow thinking we are going to be happy, or should I say fulfilled. We must set a standard and live by that standard, not settling for less. It is then, and only then that we will experience consistent breakthrough and ongoing momentum in our lives.

For all the times I settled for less than, the easy way out, or was just plain ole disobedient, it only prolonged my journey in the wilderness. I still got to the expected end, but with a lot more unnecessary heartache on my behalf. I call it "taking the scenic route."

No matter what, stay true to yourself and what God has called you to do. You will find that having consistency in this process will go a long way. Some of the ways we can stay consistent is by spending time with God, surrounding ourselves with positive people, and staying focused on the positive.

So many times, we get off on the "bunny trail" - getting involved in situations we should not be involved in. When we spend time with God, we are sensitive to His will for our lives. This allows God to download information and instruction to us. When we surround ourselves with positive people, we are energized, even more so, about our mission in life. We sharpen one another. We learn and we grow.

When we are focused, we are not pulled off our agenda every time something happens. I am not referring to remaining flexible and open to those times that God would have us to be so. I am talking about being a good steward over our time and fulfilling what God has called us to do.

Affirmation: I operate in divine timing and purpose. I am always at the right place at the right time.

Principle Three: Be True to Yourself and God

Journal Writing Prompt

Are your actions congruent with what you say you believe in?

Principle Three: Be True to Yourself and God
Journal Writing Prompt

What adjustments do you see yourself making so that you are not settling or short-changing yourself?

Principle Three: Be True to Yourself and God

Journal Writing Prompt

How can you be more consistent so that you are moving forward and operating in purpose?

Principle Three: Be True to Yourself and God
Journal Writing Prompt

What does "Being in the right place at the right time" mean to you?

Principle Four: Be Grateful for All Things

Give thanks in all circumstances; for this is God's will for you in Christ Jesus...I Thessalonians 5:18

When something happens unexpectedly to us, we oftentimes attribute it to the devil. What a blessing it is to see God in all things. When you walk and talk with God, you are able to recognize the Spirit of God moving in any situation.

It is so very important to move away from being your own worst critic. It is important not to develop a critical spirit towards yourself and/or others. When you are overly critical, you become bitter.

Nothing, absolutely nothing, can happen to you or for you unless God allows it. As you humble yourself and begin to thank God, you will begin to see things open up for you. God will allow you to see and know that the very thing that you thought was going to take you out, begin to take you up, up, and over the top. You will surely manifest what you believe.

If you would be honest with yourself, you will admit that where you are today is a result of past decisions and actions you made. Good, bad, or indifferent, you played a role in your present situation. If you do not like where you are, you must develop a way to make better decisions. It is known as making informed decisions. If you do not like where you are, you must also change your actions or the way you do things. Learn to respond rather than react.

In order to move beyond where you are, your entire attitude must change. I dare you to start thanking God for all He is and all He has allowed you to go through. This may even include where you are right now. Learn how to see the good in each and every situation and person. When you do this, not only will your mindset shift, but your *behavior* and your *attitude* will shift as well.

Affirmation: I am a grateful person. I operate in faith and not in fear.

Principle Four: Be Grateful for All Things
Journal Writing Prompt

Name five things you are grateful for?

Principle Four: Be Grateful for All Things
Journal Writing Prompt

Explain how being grateful is more beneficial to your progress than being overly critical?

Principle Four: Be Grateful for All Things
Journal Writing Prompt

Describe the environment you grew up in or the environment you presently live.

Principle Four: Be Grateful for All Things
Journal Writing Prompt

If any aspect of your environment has been critical versus affirming, how has this influenced who you are today?

Principle Four: Be Grateful for All Things
Journal Writing Prompt

What are you critical about and how do you plan to change it?

38

Principle Five: Believe Success is for You and Recognize Opportunity

Be wise in the way you act toward outsiders; make the most of every opportunity. Colossians 4:5 (NIV)

It is a small world, therefore, govern yourself accordingly. It has been said that, "There are six degrees of separation." How many times have you found yourself trying to size somebody up? Well, remember you cannot judge a book by its cover. When you are prayerful, meditating, and being watchful, your spiritual discernment will sharpen. You will not have a need to try and size people up. You will find out that God can use whomever or whatever He pleases to get you to your final destination.

Please realize that not everyone who crosses your path will act or think like you, look like you, dress like you, NOR believe like you. Many people will miss out on opportunities because they are too busy trying to size people up. I challenge you to release your biases and expectations.

Now that you have written down your goals, it would be wise to focus on them and not on people. You must see yourself already "There." It does not matter what you have done or where you have been. It does not matter what Mama and Daddy did or did not do. It does not even matter what the naysayers say. When you write down your goals according to the desires God has given you and you saturate them in prayer, you will begin to operate in your purpose.

When you are faithful in the small things, you will find yourself being elevated to the next level. All of the things I have previously mentioned come into play here as well. That includes your mindset, your attitude, and being consistent. When you write down your goals (your life vision), and you begin moving in faith, not fear, God will honor it. God will honor you. Whatever is broken, He knows how to fix it.

Affirmation: I lack no thing, and I am blessed to be a blessing.

Principle Five: Believe Success is for You and Recognize Opportunity

Journal Writing Prompt

What does success look like for you and where are you now on a scale of 1-10, with 10 being the most successful?

Principle Five: Believe Success is for You and Recognize Opportunity

Journal Writing Prompt

Sometimes we can get caught up in the day to day grind. What techniques are you implementing or willing to implement to reinforce your success and fulfill your potential?

Principle Five: Believe Success is for You and Recognize Opportunity

Journal Writing Prompt

How are you able to recognize opportunity?

Principle Five: Believe Success is for You and Recognize Opportunity

Journal Writing Prompt

Talk about how you visualize and/or see yourself as far as walking in your purpose?

Principle Six: Have Courage to Prepare

Be strong and courageous and do the work. Do not be afraid or discouraged, for the LORD God, my God, is with you... I Chronicles 28:20 (NIV)

In the past, I would sometimes wonder how I could have faith for someone else's breakthrough and then, at times, struggle to see my own. Sometimes we are very hard on ourselves because we sometimes do not see ourselves as being worthy to do what we are called to do or to have what we should have. Sometimes we are simply ***unprepared.*** It indeed takes courage to prepare, especially when you feel that you have royally messed up many times. It is even more difficult when you are in "people bondage." That means you are overly concerned about what others may think or say, or even worse, you feel you need their approval.

Don't get it confused. Being ready is not the same thing as being prepared. Let's look at it this way. One can be "ready" as in having an emotional desire to take action or to get prepared. Being "prepared" implies having to take some steps or counting the cost for a particular situation. When one is prepared, he or she has done the homework and is not moving off of a whim or pure passion. When one is prepared, he or she will (without a doubt) be committed for the journey. The Scripture declares in Proverbs 24:27 (AMP), "Establishing your priorities and proceeding in an orderly manner brings its own reward."

When one is prepared, he or she has planned and understand that going through the process of preparation is necessary. Furthermore, when one is being prepared, there will be times where aloneness may come. There may even be some distractions that crop up. However, in the process of being prepared, one will learn how to stay focused and reach his or her desired outcome. Remember, earlier I said this one was one of my past weaknesses. I encourage you to stay the course. Take courage and endure the process of preparation.

Affirmation: I am fully equipped to do what I am called to do. I am anointed and appointed.

Principle Six: Have Courage to Prepare

Journal Writing Prompt

Name 3-5 things you can do to prepare yourself in terms of your purpose. Explain your answers in detail.

Principle Six: Have Courage to Prepare

Journal Writing Prompt

What are some things that have prevented you from being courageous in times past?

Principle Six: Have Courage to Prepare

Journal Writing Prompt

How important is it for you to endure the process of preparation?

Principle Six: Have Courage to Prepare

Journal Writing Prompt

How has this chapter influenced the way you see yourself in terms of being prepared?

Principle Seven: Walk in the Fullness Thereof

The Lord will accomplish what concerns me; Your
lovingkindness, Oh Lord, is
everlasting; Do not forsake the works of Your hands.
Psalms 138:8 (NASB)

What if I were to tell you that fulfilling your destiny requires your participation? Destiny does not just happen. We as humans have the ability to make choices, and we choose rather or not we are going to agree with God and His will for our lives. We choose rather or not we are going to align and agree with heaven.

When it comes to walking in your destiny, it is necessary to operate in an intentional manner. Destiny does not just occur by happenstance. May I suggest that you pay close attention to the patterns in your life. Pay close attention to what you love to do. In fact, pay attention to where you are right now in your life journey. These are signs of your destiny.

I remember how, despite the many mistakes I have made or the many challenges I may have faced, people would frequently come to me for answers to their problems. Yes, both friends and family, and even sometimes people I did not know came to me. I would always be able to give them an answer and at this time, I was not pursuing my formal education. This is why I sometimes say, my destiny found me. Another thing I remember is that no matter how bad I may have messed up, I would continue to pray, read the Bible, and fellowship. Somehow my spiritual practices would help me regroup or refocus. I also felt encouraged and strengthened, and even at my lowest point when I wanted to give up, I couldn't. Little did I know, I was being prepared.

I remember even, in the midst of preparation, I was so "ready" to be used by God or so I thought. I also remember one of my mentors saying to me, "When you really see what God wants you to do, you are going to want to run and go in the other direction." It is so important to be accountable and be open to feedback from our mentors and teachers.

Well, let me just say that destiny is calling you and everyday may not be filled with sunshine. However, at the end of the day, there is absolutely nothing better than doing what you were born to do. When you know that you know that you know, there will not be anybody or anything that can stop you from moving forward in what God has called you to do. Let me remind you that it is a process. It may not be an easy process, but it is well worth it. There are people waiting on you.

In closing, I will say that the people God allows to be in your life such as mentors, teachers, coaches, counselors, etc., are those who can help shorten the distance as you walk in purpose to fulfill your destiny. In other words, these are the people who can help you so that you are less likely to take the scenic route. Nevertheless, enjoy the journey.

Affirmation: I am the solution to many people's problems.

Principle Seven: Walk in the Fullness Thereof
Journal Writing Prompt

Explain the difference between purpose and destiny? Now connect your purpose and destiny together as you understand it right now.

Principle Seven: Walk in the Fullness Thereof
Journal Writing Prompt

How have your choices impacted where you are now along your journey?

Principle Seven: Walk in the Fullness Thereof
Journal Writing Prompt

What changes will you make in your decision-making process?

Principle Seven: Walk in the Fullness Thereof
Journal Writing Prompt

How do you see yourself in terms of walking in your purpose?

LET WISDOM SPEAK:
KEYS to FULFILL YOUR DESTINY

Wisdom Principles & Journal

About the Author

Terry D. Gartrell is a visionary and native of Jacksonville, Florida. She has had the pleasure of traveling around the world. She is a wife, mother, and grandmother. Terry has over 30 years in public service and is passionate about helping others identify their purpose and destiny. She is the Founder of NuVision Counseling & Coaching Solutions and maintains a private practice.

Service Solutions include: Professional Counseling, Temperament Counseling, Life Coaching, Small Groups, Support Services, and Motivational Speaking. Services are provided on site in a traditional therapeutic setting. Two of the things that sets Terry apart are the mobile mental health clinic and financial training.

<u>Terry D. Gartrell, MA</u>

Mental Health Counselor
Temperament Counselor
Professional Certified Life Coach

LET WISDOM SPEAK:
KEYS to FULFILL YOUR DESTINY

Wisdom Principles & Journal

Contact Terry D. Gartrell for the following service solutions:
professional counseling, coaching, small groups, speaking engagements, and workshops

Website: www.terrydgartrell.com

Email Address: contact@terrydgartrell.com or gartrell.terry01@gmail.com

www.psychologytoday.com
(Listed as the agency not author's name)

Facebook: facebook.com/NuVision4you/

Instagram: @nuvision4you

Periscope: @tgartrell0610

Twitter: @excellentspirit

Mailing Address: 1100 Kings Road Unit 43402 Jacksonville, FL 32203

Business Line: (904)-866-2248

Made in the USA
Lexington, KY
29 November 2019